PUBLIC SPEAKING

Foundation

Fahaz Hameed

Amazon

Copyright © 2023 Amazon

All rights reserved

The characters and events portrayed in this book are fictitious. Any similarity to real persons, living or dead, is coincidental and not intended by the author.

No part of this book may be reproduced, or stored in a retrieval system, or transmitted in any form or by any means, electronic, mechanical, photocopying, recording, or otherwise, without express written permission of the publisher.

ISBN: 9798397269919

Cover design by: Fahaz Hameed

Printed in the United Arab Emirates

To my beloved mother, Kadeeja Hameed,

You have been the guiding light and pillar of strength in my life. Your unwavering love, support, and encouragement have fueled my passion for writing and exploration. This article is dedicated to you, as a token of gratitude for the endless sacrifices you have made and the boundless love you have showered upon me.

To my dear family,

Your love and unwavering support have been my foundation throughout this creative journey. This article is dedicated to each and every one of you, for being the source of inspiration and motivation in my life. Your belief in me has given me the courage to pursue my dreams and embrace the complexities of life.

May this dedication serve as a heartfelt expression of gratitude to my mother, family, and friends for their unconditional love, belief, and support. You have played an instrumental role in shaping this creative endeavor, and I am forever grateful for your presence in my life.

With deepest love and appreciation,

FAHAZ HAMEED

INTRODUCTION

In a world where silence often dominates the stage and anxiety tightens its grip on our vocal cords, there exists a remarkable art that can empower, captivate, and inspire. Welcome to the grand theater of public speaking, where words become melodies, gestures dance in harmony, and ideas take flight on the wings of eloquence.

Just as a skilled architect must lay a solid foundation for a towering masterpiece, so too must the aspiring orator build their own foundation in the realm of public speaking. But let us cast aside the traditional notions of dry textbooks and stuffy lectures, for this is a journey we embark upon with imagination as our guide and creativity as our compass.

Picture yourself standing before a crowd, the spotlight casting its warm glow upon you. Your heart races with anticipation, and a spark of excitement ignites within your soul. As you open your mouth, not only do you speak words, but you give birth to worlds. You possess the power to sway opinions, kindle emotions, and ignite change. This is the enchanting realm we shall explore together, for within these pages lies the key to unlocking your own personal charisma and commanding the stage with grace.

Prepare to delve into the secrets of the great orators, from the golden age of antiquity to the modern-day storytellers who captivate millions with their voices. Uncover the mysterious techniques that weave spells of persuasion, discover the art of connecting deeply with your audience, and unravel the hidden threads of charisma that entwine your words with influence.

But this journey is not solely for those who yearn to speak to crowds from towering podiums. Whether you aim to dazzle colleagues in boardrooms, mesmerize friends with your captivating tales, or simply conquer the demons of social anxiety, the art of public speaking will empower you. It is a foundation upon which you can build the life you desire, a gateway to confident self-expression and boundless personal growth.

So, dear reader, let us embark upon this odyssey together. Leave behind your fears and embrace the magic that awaits within these pages. Let us unfurl the wings of your voice, nourish the roots of your confidence, and watch as you soar to new heights, transforming both yourself and the world around you. The stage is set, and the curtain is about to rise on your journey through the extraordinary world of public speaking's foundation.

PREFACE

Welcome, dear reader, to a journey that will unlock the transformative power of your voice and elevate your public speaking to new heights. Within the pages of this book, we invite you to immerse yourself in the artistry of communication and explore the untapped realms of creativity that lie within you.

Public speaking is not merely a skill to be mastered; it is a form of self-expression that has the potential to inspire, influence, and ignite change. In a world where attention spans waver and information overload prevails, it is crucial to embrace unique and creative approaches to captivate your audience and leave a lasting impact.

The purpose of this book is not to provide a formulaic approach to public speaking, but rather to serve as a catalyst for your own creative exploration. Each chapter will invite you to reimagine the fundamental aspects of public speaking through a lens of innovation and originality. We will venture beyond traditional boundaries, challenging conventional wisdom and empowering you to infuse your speeches with a distinctive and memorable voice.

Drawing upon the wisdom of great orators, artists, and thinkers throughout history, we will uncover the secrets of effective communication and tap into the infinite reservoir of creativity that resides within you. Together, we will explore unique techniques to identify your audience, craft compelling messages, master your delivery, and forge a genuine connection with your listeners.

Throughout this book, you will encounter inspiring anecdotes, and practical tips to help you embrace your own creative potential. We encourage you to embark on this journey with an open mind and a willingness to step outside your comfort zone. Embrace the unexpected, challenge your assumptions, and let your imagination soar.

Remember, this book is not a definitive guide, but rather an invitation to co-create and co-discover the art of public speaking. Your voice is unique, and the world awaits your distinct perspective. By embracing the artistry of public speaking and infusing it with your creative spirit, you have the power to inspire, entertain, and transform.

As you embark on this journey, we encourage you to embrace vulnerability, embrace failure as a stepping stone to growth, and embrace your authentic self. Let your words become a symphony that resonates in the hearts and minds of your audience. Together, let us unleash the power of unique and creative expression and elevate the art of public speaking to new horizons.

So, dear reader, prepare to embark on a remarkable expedition. Embrace the artistry of public speaking and discover the limitless possibilities that lie within. The stage is set, the audience awaits, and your voice is ready to soar. Let us begin this prelude to unique and creative expression.

PROLOGUE

The hushed anticipation lingers in the air, as the velvet curtains slowly part to reveal a stage bathed in warm light. The orchestra's melody whispers in the background, setting the mood for an extraordinary performance about to unfold. In this grand theater of public speaking, where words have the power to mesmerize, inspire, and shape destinies, we find ourselves at the threshold of a transformative journey.

Welcome to the prologue of a book that invites you to step into the spotlight and embrace the art of unique and creative expression. Like a masterful overture, this prologue sets the stage for the symphony of public speaking that will unfold in the chapters that follow.

On this stage, we break free from the shackles of convention and venture into uncharted territory. We challenge the norms, question the established practices, and encourage you, the reader, to unleash the untapped potential of your own voice. It is within this sacred space of creative exploration that true artistry is born.

In the pages ahead, you will discover that public speaking is not limited to a rigid set of rules or a one-size-fits-all approach. Instead, it is a vibrant canvas where your unique experiences, passions, and perspectives intertwine to create something truly extraordinary. Each speech you deliver becomes a masterpiece, carefully crafted and passionately presented.

We invite you to embark on a journey of self-discovery, where you will learn to harness the power of creativity, authenticity, and connection. Through the stories of great orators, poets, and visionaries, we will explore the transformative impact of unique and creative expression. We will delve into the nuances of body language, vocal variety, and storytelling techniques that bring your words to life.

This prologue serves as an invitation to step beyond the boundaries of traditional public speaking and embrace a new paradigm. It is an invitation to discover your own voice, to tap into the wellspring of creativity that lies within, and to honor the power of authentic self-expression.

As you turn the pages that lie before you, remember that the stage is set, and you are the protagonist of your own speaking journey. Embrace the vulnerability of sharing your ideas, the exhilaration of captivating an audience, and the profound impact your words can have on others.

Dear reader, as the curtains draw closer, let us embark on this extraordinary voyage together. The world eagerly awaits the unique and creative expression that only you can bring. The stage is set, the audience is waiting, and it is time for your voice to shine. Let the prologue unfold, and let the symphony of public speaking begin.

PREPARE YOUR SPEECH

CHAPTER 1

Unveiling the Mysterious Faces in the Crowd: Mastering the Art of Audience Identification

In the magical realm of public speaking, the audience becomes the protagonist in the grand theater of your performance. They hold the key to your success, their reactions shaping the very fabric of your presentation. But who are these enigmatic individuals who gather to witness your oratorical prowess? Welcome to the unveiling of the mysterious faces in the crowd, where we embark on a quest to master the art of audience identification like never before.

Picture a bustling masquerade ball, where each attendee dons a unique mask, concealing their true identities. As the host of this extraordinary event, your mission is to peel away those masks, revealing the diverse characters that await your captivating words. It is not enough to merely know that they exist; you must truly understand them, connecting with their deepest desires, fears, and aspirations.

So, don your cloak of curiosity, and let us journey together through the labyrinth of audience identification. Here, we shall explore unconventional methods, defying the ordinary to uncover the extraordinary. For it is not merely demographics and statistics that define our audience; it is the intangible threads that weave the tapestry of their souls.

Step into the shoes of an anthropologist, observing the customs, quirks, and nuances of your audience. Explore the landscapes of their lives, seeking out their passions, interests, and pain points. Engage in conversations, whether virtual or face-to-face, to truly listen and empathize with their experiences.

But let us venture even deeper, for our audience is not a monolithic entity. Within the crowd, there exist subcultures, each with their own language, symbols, and dreams. Unearth these hidden tribes and learn their ways, for they hold the keys to connection and resonance.

Embrace the power of storytelling, for within the narratives lie the secrets to capturing the hearts and minds of your audience. Craft tales that mirror their struggles and triumphs, weaving a tapestry of empathy that envelops them in your words. Transport them to distant lands, evoke emotions that stir their souls, and paint vivid pictures that ignite their imaginations.

And as you embark on this quest, never forget the power of authenticity. Be genuine, for your audience can sense the façade of insincerity from miles away. Let your passion radiate through your words, for it is the fire that kindles the flames within their hearts.

So, fellow traveler in the realm of public speaking, let us embark on this exhilarating expedition together. Unveil the mysterious faces in the crowd, connect with their souls, and transform your presentations into profound experiences. Through the art of audience identification, we shall forge a bond that transcends the barriers of time and space. Are you ready to step into the spotlight and captivate those who await your wisdom? The journey begins now.

CHAPTER 2

Unveiling the Purpose Within: Discovering the Essence of Your Voice

In the vast landscape of public speaking, where words can soar like eagles or crumble like sandcastles, there lies a hidden gem that holds the power to elevate your presence from mere speaker to a beacon of inspiration. Welcome to the exploration of the essence within, as we embark on a journey to uncover the depths of your purpose and unravel the intricate tapestry of why you are talking like never before.

Imagine a labyrinth, adorned with mirrors reflecting the myriad possibilities of your voice. As you navigate this maze, let us shed the conventional notions of surface-level motivations and delve into the core of your being. It is here, amidst the echoes of your aspirations and dreams, that you will find the true source of your power.

At the heart of every remarkable speaker lies a profound understanding of their purpose. It is not merely about sharing information or entertaining the masses; it is about connecting with something greater than oneself. So, let us embark on this transformative quest, peering through the kaleidoscope of possibilities to reveal the essence that fuels your voice.

Gaze into the mirror of self-reflection and ask yourself, "Why do I speak?" Is it to spark change, to challenge the status quo, or to give voice to the voiceless? Perhaps it is to inspire, to ignite hope in the hearts of others, or to share wisdom that has been bestowed upon you. Whatever the reason, it is essential to unearth the true essence that drives you to stand before the crowd.

But let us journey deeper still, for your purpose is not isolated from the world around you. It intertwines with the collective yearnings, struggles, and aspirations of humanity. Explore the vast landscapes of society, and ask yourself, "How can my voice contribute to the greater good?" Identify the pressing issues, the unmet needs, and the transformative potential that aligns with your purpose.

Embrace the art of storytelling once more, for it is through narratives that we can touch the hearts and minds of others. Craft tales that embody the essence of your purpose, painting vivid pictures of a world transformed. Allow your words to transcend the mundane and soar to the realm of possibility, inviting others to join you on this remarkable journey.

As you uncover the essence within, never forget the power of authenticity. Your voice is unique, and it resonates with a timbre that no one else possesses. Embrace your quirks, your vulnerabilities, and your passions, for they are the brushstrokes that paint the masterpiece of your purpose.

So, fellow seeker of the essence within, let us embark on this extraordinary voyage together. Unveil the layers of why you are talking, and let your purpose shine like a guiding star in the night sky. Embrace the transformative power of your voice and become a catalyst for change. Are you ready to discover the essence that propels you forward? The journey awaits.

CHAPTER 3

The Art of Architectural Oratory: Sculpting the Blueprint of Your Speech

In the realm of public speaking, where words take flight and ideas dance upon the air, lies a remarkable tool that separates the ordinary from the extraordinary. Welcome to the enchanting world of architectural oratory, where we unlock the secrets of sculpting a speech that resonates deeply with your audience. Step into the shoes of a master architect as we explore the unique and creative process of outlining your speech.

Imagine yourself in a vast gallery, surrounded by vibrant canvases and intricate sculptures. Each artwork tells a story, evoking emotions and stirring the soul. Now, envision your speech as a masterpiece in progress, waiting to be shaped by your artistic vision. It is within this gallery of inspiration that we begin our journey.

Release the constraints of traditional outlines and let your imagination run wild. Embrace the power of unconventional structures, for it is through creativity that your speech will truly come alive. Draw inspiration from the avant-garde, the surreal, and the unexpected, infusing your outline with a touch of artistic brilliance.

Consider your speech as a grand symphony, with each section flowing seamlessly into the next. Begin with a captivating overture, an attention-grabbing introduction that sets the tone for what is to come. Paint vivid strokes of imagery, allowing your audience to see, feel, and experience your words.

Now, let us delve into the body of your speech, the core of your message. Think of it as a labyrinth of interconnected ideas, where each path leads to a revelation. Embrace the power of contrast, juxtaposing opposing viewpoints or weaving together seemingly unrelated concepts. Allow your outline to be a tapestry of complexity, where the threads of your ideas intertwine and create a mesmerizing whole.

As you shape your outline, remember the importance of rhythm and pacing. Just as a symphony has its crescendos and diminuendos, so too should your speech ebb and flow. Build suspense, pause for emphasis, and let the silence speak volumes. It is within these moments of anticipation that your words will truly resonate with your audience.

And finally, the conclusion, the grand finale of your speech. Think of it as a breathtaking tableau, leaving your audience in awe and yearning for more. Summarize your main points with eloquence, reinforce your message with conviction, and end with a memorable call to action that inspires and empowers.

But amidst this creative process, do not forget the importance of clarity and coherence. Your outline should serve as a roadmap, guiding you through the labyrinth of your ideas. Ensure that your main points are clear, your transitions are smooth, and your structure is easy to follow. Balance the artistic flourishes with a strong foundation of organization and logic.

So, fellow architect of oratory, let us embark on this creative journey together. Embrace the artistic freedom that awaits you, and sculpt an outline that transcends the boundaries of tradition. Let your speech become a masterpiece that captivates and moves your audience. Are you ready to unleash your creative genius and shape a speech that will leave an indelible mark? The canvas awaits your touch.

CHAPTER 4

Unearthing the Treasures Within: Unleashing the Power of Your Unique Storytelling

In the boundless realm of public speaking, where stories become windows into the human experience, lies a hidden trove of riches waiting to be discovered. Welcome to the journey of unearthing the treasures within, as we dive deep into the art of finding your story in a unique and creative way. Prepare to embark on an extraordinary adventure, where the ordinary becomes extraordinary, and your voice becomes a beacon of authenticity.

Imagine yourself as an archeologist, equipped with a keen eye and a thirst for discovery. Your mission is to unearth the gems hidden within your own life, experiences, and imagination. Cast aside the notion that your story is ordinary or unworthy, for within the depths of your being lie treasures waiting to be shared.

Let us venture beyond the traditional narratives and embrace the unconventional. Explore the vivid dreams that visit you in the realm of slumber, the whimsical musings that dance in the corners of your mind, and the tales whispered by the winds of your soul. Give voice to the fragments of your imagination, weaving them into stories that captivate and inspire.

Unearth the emotions that reside within your heart, for they are the fuel that ignites the flames of connection. Embrace vulnerability and authenticity, for it is through these elements that your story becomes relatable and powerful. Share the triumphs, the struggles, and the lessons learned along your journey, allowing others to see themselves reflected in your words.

But do not limit yourself to the confines of your own experiences. Embrace the gift of empathy and step into the shoes of others. Seek out stories that exist beyond your own, whether from history, literature, or the lives of those around you. Let these stories become a tapestry of inspiration, enriching your own narrative and expanding the horizons of your audience.

Just as an artist selects the perfect brushstroke or a musician plays the right note, craft your storytelling techniques with intention and flair. Experiment with the power of vivid imagery, painting pictures with your words that transport your audience to different worlds. Use the rhythm of your speech to create an immersive experience, evoking emotions and engaging their senses.

Remember that your story is not solely about you; it is a gift to your audience. Tailor your storytelling to their needs, desires, and aspirations. Weave threads of universal themes that resonate with their hearts and minds, touching upon the shared human experience that binds us all. Your story becomes a bridge that connects souls and builds a sense of belonging.

So, fellow storyteller extraordinaire, let us embark on this grand adventure together. Unearth the treasures within and give voice to the tales that only you can tell. Embrace the power of creativity and authenticity, infusing your storytelling with a touch of magic. Are you ready to captivate, inspire, and leave an indelible mark on the hearts of your audience? The world eagerly awaits your story.

BEFORE YOUR SPEECH

CHAPTER 5

Igniting the Inner Flame: Unleashing Your Unique Warm-Up Rituals

I n the vibrant realm of public speaking, where words become the currency of connection, lies a sacred ritual that fuels the fires of your voice. Welcome to the enchanting exploration of warming up before speaking, where we unlock the secrets of preparing your mind, body, and spirit in a unique and creative way. Step into the realm of imagination and unleash your inner flame.

Imagine a theater backstage, a haven of anticipation and energy. Here, you have the opportunity to cultivate a warm-up ritual that is as unique as you are. Cast aside the notion of routine warm-ups and embrace a tapestry of practices that ignite your spirit and empower your voice.

Begin by reconnecting with your breath, the life force that sustains you. Breathe deeply, inhaling the essence of possibility and exhaling any tension or doubt. Let your breath become a gentle breeze that clears the stage for your performance, allowing you to enter the spotlight with a sense of calm and presence.

Embrace the power of movement, for your body is an instrument that amplifies your words. Engage in a dance of liberation, allowing your limbs to stretch, sway, and flow. Shake off any stagnant energy and invite vitality to course through your veins. Let your movements reflect the cadence of your speech, embodying the rhythm and expression of your words.

Now, let us tap into the realm of the senses, for they are the gateway to connection and engagement. Engage your sense of touch by feeling the texture of an object that resonates with your message—a smooth stone, a velvety fabric, or the rough bark of a tree. Allow this tactile experience to anchor you in the present moment, grounding your presence on stage.

Enliven your auditory senses by listening to music that stirs your emotions and uplifts your spirit. Let the melodies transport you to a state of inspiration and ignite the fire within. Allow the harmonies and rhythms to infuse your being, guiding your voice and infusing your speech with a symphony of passion.

Embrace the power of visualization, painting vivid mental pictures of success and connection. See yourself on the stage, radiating confidence, and connecting deeply with your audience. Visualize the positive impact your words will have, the transformations they will inspire, and the memories they will create. Let this visualization become an anchor of motivation and purpose.

Lastly, cultivate a moment of stillness and reflection. Find a quiet space within yourself, where the noise of the outside world fades away. Close your eyes and tune in to the whispers of your intuition, the wisdom that guides you. Trust in your unique voice and the messages that seek expression through you.

Remember, dear speaker, that your warm-up ritual is a personal journey of discovery and self-expression. Embrace the power of creativity and intuition as you craft your unique warm-up practice. Let it become a sacred dance that prepares you to step onto the stage and share your voice with the world.

So, fellow igniter of the inner flame, let us embark on this magical exploration together. Unleash your unique warm-up rituals and cultivate a state of readiness that is both vibrant and serene. Are you ready to step into the spotlight, knowing that you have prepared yourself from the inside out? The stage awaits your radiant presence.

CHAPTER 6

Embrace the Magic Mic: A Journey of Empowerment and Collaboration

In the enchanting realm of public speaking, where words hold the power to transform lives, lies a magical artifact that awaits your touch. Welcome to the extraordinary journey of saying yes to the microphone, where we delve into the realms of empowerment and collaboration in a unique and creative way. Prepare to embark on a wondrous adventure, where the microphone becomes your ally, and your voice resonates with undeniable strength.

Imagine a mystical ceremony, where the microphone stands as a symbol of empowerment and connection. As you approach, a surge of anticipation fills the air, for this moment is about more than amplifying your voice. It is an invitation to step into your true power, to embrace the collective energy of the audience, and to create a magical exchange of ideas and emotions.

Take a moment to acknowledge the microphone as a potent talisman, carrying the stories and voices of those who came before you. Each time it is handed to you, a torch is passed, an opportunity to leave an indelible mark on the hearts and minds of your listeners. Embrace this sacred trust and feel the energy of all who have stood before you, amplifying their voices through this magical conduit.

As you hold the microphone in your hand, feel its weight, its presence. Let it serve as a reminder of your own power and authority. Say yes to the microphone, for in doing so, you affirm your readiness to share your unique message and perspective with the world. It becomes a vessel for your voice to reverberate through the hearts of those who listen.

But remember, the microphone is not just a tool for solo performance. It is a gateway to collaboration and connection. Embrace the opportunity to engage in a dance of dialogue with your audience. Allow the microphone to become a bridge that spans the distance between speaker and listener, inviting them to lean in, to feel seen and heard.

Consider the microphone as a magical wand, capable of amplifying not only your voice but also the voices of others. Use it to uplift and empower those around you, inviting them to share their thoughts, perspectives, and stories. Create an environment where every voice is valued, where the symphony of ideas intertwines and harmonizes.

When you say yes to the microphone, you say yes to vulnerability. Embrace the raw and authentic parts of yourself, for they are the catalysts for connection and empathy. Share your triumphs and struggles, your fears and aspirations. Open yourself up to the transformative power of vulnerability, and watch as your audience leans in, captivated by your authenticity.

And as you stand before the microphone, remember that it is not just about the words you speak. It is about the energy, the presence, and the intention that you bring. Let your voice carry the melody of passion, your words dance with conviction, and your energy radiate with purpose. Feel the magic flow through you as you surrender to the moment.

So, fellow magician of the microphone, let us embark on this enchanting journey together. Embrace the power, the connection, and the collaboration that awaits you. Say yes to the microphone, and watch as your voice weaves its magic through the hearts of all who listen. Are you ready to step into your power and create an unforgettable experience? The microphone eagerly awaits your embrace.

CHAPTER 7

Taming the Inner Tempest: Transforming Pre-Performance Anxiety into Fuel for Success

In the realm of public speaking, where words hold the power to inspire and captivate, lies a formidable adversary that many face: pre-performance anxiety. But fear not, for within this chapter, we embark on a unique and creative journey of managing and transforming pre-performance anxiety into fuel for success. Brace yourself as we unlock the secrets to taming the inner tempest and unleashing your true potential.

Imagine yourself standing on the edge of a precipice, a swirling storm of nerves and anticipation brewing within. But instead of succumbing to the tempest, let us harness its energy and transform it into a force that propels you forward. Embrace the creative tools at your disposal and embark on a transformative journey of managing pre-performance anxiety.

Enter the realm of mindfulness, where the present moment becomes your sanctuary. Engage in deep breathing exercises, allowing each inhale to anchor you in the here and now, and each exhale to release tension and doubt. Embrace the power of meditation, finding stillness within the chaos, and cultivating a sense of calm that permeates your being.

Visualize your anxiety as a vibrant flame, flickering with intensity. Instead of extinguishing it, imagine channeling that fiery energy into a laser-like focus. Let it burn away any distractions and doubts, leaving behind only the essence of your passion and purpose. Embrace the idea that your anxiety is a sign of your investment, a testament to your desire to deliver an impactful performance.

Embrace the power of creative expression as a means to manage anxiety. Engage in journaling, where you pour your thoughts and fears onto the page, releasing their hold on your mind. Explore the realms of art, music, or dance, allowing these creative outlets to channel your anxiety into something beautiful and transformative. Let your creativity be the brush that paints a vivid tapestry of confidence and resilience.

Seek out a trusted confidant, a supportive ally who can lend an empathetic ear and offer words of encouragement. Share your anxieties and fears, allowing their presence to be acknowledged and validated. Together, explore coping strategies and techniques that resonate with your unique needs. The power of connection and understanding can be a soothing balm for the anxious soul.

Embrace the power of positive affirmations, for they are the shield that guards against self-doubt. Craft mantras that remind you of your strengths, your resilience, and your ability to overcome challenges. Repeat them with conviction, allowing their truth to resonate within you. Transform your inner dialogue into a symphony of self-empowerment and belief.

Engage in physical movement to release the pent-up energy that anxiety brings. Take a brisk walk, practice yoga, or engage in a playful dance. Let your body become a vessel for the release of tension, freeing your mind and spirit from the grip of anxiety. Embrace the power of physicality and let it ground you in the present moment.

Remember, dear speaker, that pre-performance anxiety is not an enemy to be defeated but a companion to be embraced. It is a testament to your passion, your investment, and your commitment to delivering your best. By transforming anxiety into fuel, you tap into an inner reservoir of strength and resilience that propels you towards success.

So, fellow conqueror of the inner tempest, let us embark on this transformative journey together. Embrace the power of mindfulness, creativity, connection, and movement to manage pre-performance anxiety. Harness its energy and let it propel you to new heights. Are you ready to tame the tempest and step onto the stage with confidence and grace? The world eagerly awaits your transformative performance.

CHAPTER 8

The Dance of Mastery: Unleashing Creativity in Speech Rehearsals

In the realm of public speaking, where words become an intricate dance of connection and impact, lies a transformative practice awaiting your embrace: rehearsing your speech. But let us venture beyond the traditional notions of rehearsing and explore a unique and creative approach that unleashes the full potential of your message. Get ready to step onto the stage of mastery and infuse your rehearsals with creativity and passion.

Imagine your rehearsal space as a blank canvas, a sanctuary where you can paint the vibrant strokes of your speech. Release the notion of rote memorization and embrace a dynamic process that brings your words to life. Let us embark on a journey of exploration and self-expression that turns rehearsals into an art form.

Begin by infusing your space with inspiration. Surround yourself with visual cues that evoke the essence of your message—photographs, artwork, or objects that resonate with the emotions you seek to convey. Let these reminders envelop you, fueling your imagination and setting the stage for a rehearsal that transcends mere repetition.

Experiment with different modes of expression. Instead of standing stationary and reciting your words, explore the power of movement. Let your body become an instrument of storytelling, using gestures, postures, and physicality to enhance the impact of your message. Allow the rhythm of your speech to guide your movements, creating a seamless flow between your words and actions.

Engage in role-playing exercises to embody different perspectives and characters within your speech. Step into their shoes, adopting their mannerisms, vocal tones, and emotions. By fully immersing yourself in the roles, you gain a deeper understanding of the diverse voices within your speech, enriching your delivery and connecting with your audience on a profound level.

Embrace the power of improvisation. Set aside the script for a moment and allow yourself to explore spontaneous moments of creativity. Let your mind and words wander, trusting in your ability to adapt and respond in the moment. This practice strengthens your flexibility as a speaker, empowering you to navigate unexpected twists and turns with grace.

Integrate technology and multimedia elements into your rehearsals. Embrace the power of visual aids, slides, or videos that enhance the impact of your message. Use sound effects or music to create a multisensory experience that immerses your audience in the heart of your narrative. Leverage the tools available to you to amplify the power of your delivery.

Collaborate with others during your rehearsals. Seek feedback from trusted individuals who can offer fresh perspectives and insights. Engage in dialogue, inviting them to share their interpretations and suggestions. Embrace the collective wisdom and diverse viewpoints that arise from collaboration, allowing them to shape and refine your speech.

Capture the essence of your rehearsals through creative mediums. Consider recording audio or video of your practice sessions. Reviewing these recordings allows you to observe your delivery, identify areas for improvement, and witness the evolution of your performance. It also serves as a source of inspiration and a record of your growth as a speaker.

Remember, dear speaker, that rehearsing your speech is not just about memorization or mechanical repetition. It is an invitation to unleash your creativity, to breathe life into your words, and to connect with your audience in profound ways. Embrace the power of imagination, movement, improvisation, collaboration, and technology as you craft a rehearsal process that is uniquely yours.

So, fellow artist of the spoken word, let us embark on this creative journey together. Infuse your rehearsals with a sense of wonder and exploration. Embrace the canvas of your rehearsal space and paint the masterpiece of your speech. Are you ready to dance the dance of mastery and unleash your creative spirit on the stage? The world eagerly awaits your captivating performance.

OPEN YOUR VOICE

CHAPTER 9

The Tapestry of Trust: Unleashing Your Authentic Credibility

In the enchanting realm of public speaking, where trust weaves the fabric of connection, lies a transformative quest: developing credibility as a speaker. But let us embark on a unique and creative journey that transcends conventional notions of credibility. Prepare to unleash the power of your authenticity, weaving a tapestry of trust that captivates and resonates with your audience.

Imagine yourself as an artist, standing before a blank canvas, ready to paint the portrait of your credibility. Release the desire for external validation and instead, dive deep into the essence of who you are. Authenticity becomes the brush with which you craft your masterpiece, revealing the colors of your experience, knowledge, and passion.

Embrace the power of storytelling as a means to establish credibility. Share personal anecdotes and narratives that illustrate your journey and expertise. Allow your audience to step into the moments that shaped you, igniting empathy and forging a connection based on shared experiences. Your stories become the threads that weave the tapestry of trust.

Let vulnerability become your superpower. Share moments of growth, setbacks, and lessons learned. Embrace the raw and authentic parts of your journey, for they become touchstones of relatability. By showcasing your humanity, you invite your audience to join you on a path of discovery, fostering an atmosphere of trust and mutual understanding.

Honor the power of active listening. Engage with your audience, seeking to understand their needs, concerns, and aspirations. Encourage dialogue and create space for diverse perspectives to be heard. By genuinely listening, you demonstrate respect and empathy, building a foundation of trust that strengthens your credibility as a speaker.

Embrace continuous learning and growth. Demonstrate your commitment to staying informed and up-to-date in your field. Share insights, research, and valuable resources that showcase your dedication to expanding your knowledge base. By nurturing your own intellectual curiosity, you inspire confidence and establish yourself as a trusted authority.

Leverage the power of visual storytelling. Craft captivating visuals that enhance the impact of your message. Embrace creative design, imagery, and infographics to communicate complex ideas with clarity and elegance. By embracing visual storytelling, you engage multiple senses and create a memorable experience that reinforces your credibility.

Cultivate a genuine passion for your topic. Let your enthusiasm radiate from within, infusing every word and gesture. Share your deep-rooted love for your subject matter, and inspire others to share in your passion. Authentic passion serves as a magnet, drawing your audience closer and establishing you as a credible and influential voice.

Build a community of trust and support. Seek out opportunities to collaborate and connect with other experts in your field. Engage in conversations, workshops, and networking events that foster a sense of camaraderie and shared knowledge. By surrounding yourself with like-minded individuals, you enrich your credibility and create a network of support.

Embrace the power of authenticity as you develop your credibility as a speaker. Release the need for perfection and embrace your unique voice, perspectives, and experiences. It is through your authenticity that you forge connections that transcend mere words, leaving an indelible mark on the hearts and minds of your audience.

So, fellow weaver of trust, let us embark on this creative journey together. Unleash your authentic self and craft a tapestry of credibility that resonates with your audience. Are you ready to paint your masterpiece and establish yourself as a trusted and influential speaker? The world eagerly awaits your genuine presence on the stage.

CHAPTER 10

Unveiling the Curtain: Five Captivating Openings to Enchant Your Audience

In the captivating realm of public speaking, where first impressions linger like the sweetest of melodies, lies the art of crafting a compelling opening. But let us transcend the ordinary and embark on a unique and creative journey that unveils the curtain of anticipation. Prepare to explore five enchanting openings that will captivate your audience from the very first moment.

Opening 1:

The Intriguing Question

Imagine stepping onto the stage and presenting your audience with a thought-provoking question that hangs in the air like a riddle waiting to be solved. Engage their curiosity, inviting them on a journey of discovery. Embrace the power of the unknown and ignite their minds, laying the groundwork for an engaging and interactive experience.

Opening 2:

The Evocative Story

Picture yourself weaving a tapestry of words, painting vivid images that transport your audience to a different time and place. Begin with a captivating story, a tale that evokes emotions and resonates with universal experiences. Allow your listeners to immerse themselves in the narrative, forging an immediate connection and setting the stage for a transformative journey.

Opening 3:
The Surprising Statistic

Imagine delivering a startling statistic or mind-boggling fact that challenges conventional thinking. Capture your audience's attention with a powerful number that unveils a hidden truth or shines a new light on a familiar topic. This opening creates an instant sense of relevance and urgency, leaving your audience hungry for more knowledge and insights.

Opening 4:
The Provocative Statement

Envision yourself standing tall and boldly declaring a provocative statement that challenges the status quo. Stir the waters of conventional wisdom, sparking a debate within the minds of your listeners. By pushing boundaries and presenting a fresh perspective, you ignite a fire of curiosity and engagement, setting the stage for a thought-provoking and memorable presentation.

Opening 5:
The Engaging Demonstration

Picture yourself stepping onto the stage with a captivating prop or a tangible object that represents the core of your message. Engage your audience's senses and demonstrate the essence of your topic through a hands-on experience. By immersing them in a tangible demonstration, you awaken their curiosity and create an instant connection that invites them to delve deeper into your presentation.

Remember, dear speaker, that the opening of your speech is the gateway to the hearts and minds of your audience. Embrace the power of intrigue, storytelling, surprising statistics, provocative statements, and engaging demonstrations to captivate your listeners from the very first moment.

So, fellow maestro of the stage, let us embark on this creative journey together. Experiment with these enchanting openings and adapt them to fit your unique style and message. Are you ready to pull back the curtain and mesmerize your audience from the first breath? The world eagerly awaits your captivating opening, setting the stage for an unforgettable performance.

CHAPTER 11

The Map to Enlightenment: Unveiling Your Agenda with Creativity and Purpose

In the realm of public speaking, where clarity and structure guide the way, lies a unique opportunity to introduce your agenda in a manner that captivates and engages your audience. Let us embark on a creative journey that unveils the map to enlightenment, igniting curiosity and setting the stage for a transformative experience. Prepare to introduce your agenda with a touch of creativity and purpose.

Imagine yourself as a guide, leading your audience on an exhilarating expedition through the vast landscape of knowledge and ideas. Embrace the power of storytelling and paint a vivid picture of the journey that awaits. Describe the destinations, the milestones, and the transformative experiences that lie ahead. By framing your agenda as an epic adventure, you awaken a sense of anticipation and excitement.

Embrace the power of metaphor and analogy to communicate your agenda. Draw parallels to familiar concepts, objects, or experiences that resonate with your audience. Paint a picture of your agenda as a tapestry of interconnected ideas, each thread contributing to the grand design. By using metaphors, you provide a visual and emotional anchor that helps your audience navigate the terrain of your presentation.

Harness the power of multimedia to introduce your agenda. Create a visually stunning video or slideshow that showcases the key elements of your agenda in an engaging and captivating way. Incorporate music, animation, or graphics that evoke the emotions and themes of your presentation. By leveraging the power of multimedia, you create a multisensory experience that leaves a lasting impression.

Infuse your agenda with interactive elements. Instead of simply listing the topics you'll cover, invite your audience to actively participate in shaping the journey. Pose questions, conduct mini-polls, or incorporate interactive exercises that allow your listeners to contribute their thoughts and insights. By involving them in the agenda-setting process, you foster a sense of ownership and engagement.

Create a visual representation of your agenda using a unique and creative format. Consider using a mind map, a flowchart, or even a physical artifact that symbolizes the progression of your presentation. By presenting your agenda in a visually compelling way, you provide a clear and memorable roadmap for your audience to follow.

Weave a narrative thread that connects the different elements of your agenda. Introduce recurring themes or motifs that serve as guideposts throughout your presentation. By establishing a narrative arc, you create a cohesive and engaging experience for your audience, making each topic and idea feel like an integral part of a larger story.

Remember, dear speaker, that introducing your agenda is more than a mere formality. It is an opportunity to ignite curiosity, engage your audience, and set the tone for an enlightening journey. Embrace the power of storytelling, metaphor, multimedia, interactivity, visual representation, and narrative threading as you introduce your agenda with creativity and purpose.

So, fellow navigator of knowledge, let us embark on this creative journey together. Unveil your agenda with a sense of adventure and purpose. Are you ready to guide your audience through the map to enlightenment, awakening their curiosity and igniting their passion for discovery? The world eagerly awaits your captivating introduction, setting the stage for an unforgettable exploration of ideas.

CHAPTER 12

Unleashing the Power of First Impressions: A Journey Beyond Common Opening Mistakes

In the enchanting realm of public speaking, where first impressions linger like a delicate dance, lies the art of avoiding common opening mistakes. But let us transcend the ordinary and embark on a unique and creative journey that empowers you to make an indelible mark from the very first moment. Prepare to unveil the secrets of captivating openings and steer clear of the pitfalls that can hinder your connection with the audience.

Mistake 1:

The Sleep-Inducing Introduction

Imagine stepping onto the stage and captivating your audience with an opening that defies the expected. Break free from the monotonous norm of lengthy, self-indulgent introductions. Instead, ignite their curiosity with a surprising fact, an intriguing quote, or a captivating anecdote. By capturing their attention from the outset, you create an atmosphere of engagement and set the stage for a dynamic exchange of ideas.

Mistake 2:

The Information Overload

Picture yourself standing tall and resisting the urge to overwhelm your audience with a barrage of information. Instead, select a few key points that encapsulate the essence of your message. Craft a concise and compelling opening that provides a glimpse into the transformative journey you are about to embark upon. By leaving room for curiosity and discovery, you invite your audience to actively participate in the unfolding narrative.

Mistake 3:

The Lackluster Opener

Envision yourself embracing the power of emotion, infusing your opening with energy and passion. Steer clear of starting with a mundane and uninspiring statement. Instead, tap into your own enthusiasm and convey the genuine excitement you feel about your topic. Let your words resonate with emotion, drawing your audience into the experience and compelling them to lean in and listen attentively.

Mistake 4:

The Preaching Monologue

Imagine engaging in a dialogue rather than delivering a one-sided monologue. Avoid launching into a lecture that distances you from your audience. Instead, pose thought-provoking questions or invite brief interactions that encourage participation. Foster a sense of connection by acknowledging the collective knowledge and experiences in the room. By creating a conversational atmosphere, you establish a foundation of trust and engagement.

Mistake 5:

The Lack of Relevance

Picture yourself customizing your opening to suit the specific needs and interests of your audience. Avoid the trap of presenting generic information that fails to resonate with them. Instead, conduct thorough research and understand the unique context of your listeners. Tailor your opening to address their challenges, aspirations, or desires. By demonstrating relevance, you establish yourself as a speaker who truly understands and empathizes with their concerns.

Mistake 6:

The Absence of Confidence

Envision yourself stepping onto the stage with unwavering confidence, radiating an aura of authenticity and poise. Avoid the mistake of starting timidly or apologizing for any perceived shortcomings. Instead, embrace your expertise and present yourself as a credible and confident speaker. Project your voice, maintain eye contact, and speak with conviction. By exuding confidence, you captivate your audience and instill trust in your abilities.

Remember, dear speaker, that the opening moments of your speech are an opportunity to forge a powerful connection with your audience. Embrace the power of surprise, concise messaging, emotion, dialogue, relevance, and confidence to avoid common opening mistakes and create a lasting impression.

So, fellow weaver of captivating openings, let us embark on this creative journey together. Break free from the common pitfalls and unleash the power of your first impression. Are you ready to captivate your audience from the very first moment, setting the stage for an unforgettable experience? The world eagerly awaits your unique and captivating opening, leaving an indelible mark on the hearts and minds of your listeners.

DELIVER YOUR SPEECH

CHAPTER 13

The Symphony of Your Voice: Unleashing Vocal Variety

In the captivating realm of public speaking, where words dance and melodies unfold, lies the art of developing vocal variety. But let us transcend the ordinary and embark on a unique and creative journey that elevates your voice to new heights. Prepare to unleash the symphony of your voice, captivating your audience with a mesmerizing array of tones, rhythms, and emotions.

Imagine your voice as a versatile instrument, capable of producing an enchanting array of sounds and expressions. Embrace the power of storytelling and use your voice to breathe life into the characters and narratives you share. Infuse each word with emotion, adjusting your tone, volume, and pace to reflect the mood and intensity of the story. Transport your audience into a world of imagination, where your voice becomes a portal to extraordinary experiences.

Experiment with the range of your vocal pitch. Like a skilled musician, explore the high and low notes of your voice to convey different meanings and intentions. Use higher pitches to express excitement, enthusiasm, or urgency. Embrace lower pitches to convey seriousness, authority, or mystery. By mastering the range of your voice, you create a captivating symphony that resonates with your listeners.

Embrace the rhythm and cadence of language. Like a conductor guiding an orchestra, use pauses, emphasis, and pacing to create a dynamic and engaging performance. Harness the power of silence to build anticipation, emphasize key points, or allow your audience to reflect. Vary your pacing to match the energy and intensity of your message, creating a rhythmic flow that holds your listeners spellbound.

Play with vocal inflections and accents. Immerse yourself in the characters and cultures you wish to portray, allowing your voice to transform and adapt. Experiment with regional accents, dialects, or even impersonations to add a touch of flair and authenticity to your delivery. By embracing the rich tapestry of vocal nuances, you bring diversity and liveliness to your presentations.

Use vocal dynamics to convey emotion and meaning. Embrace the power of volume, seamlessly transitioning between softer and louder tones to create impact and capture attention. Employ crescendos and decrescendos to add depth and intensity to your words. Let your voice become an instrument of expression, painting a vivid emotional landscape that resonates with your audience.

Employ vocal variety strategically to highlight key points and create memorable moments. Raise your voice to emphasize important concepts or ideas. Lower your voice to create a sense of intimacy or mystery. Slow down to allow your audience to absorb profound insights, and speed up to generate excitement or urgency. By consciously incorporating vocal variety, you create moments that linger in the minds of your listeners.

Remember, dear speaker, that your voice is a powerful tool waiting to be unleashed. Embrace the power of storytelling, pitch variation, rhythm, inflections, accents, dynamics, and strategic usage to develop vocal variety that captivates and inspires.

So, fellow conductor of words, let us embark on this creative journey together. Explore the symphony of your voice, unlocking its full potential. Are you ready to captivate your audience with the mesmerizing melodies and harmonies that flow from within you? The world eagerly awaits the enchanting symphony of your unique and creative vocal variety.

CHAPTER 14

Liberating Your Language: Unleashing Unique and Creative Strategies to Reduce Crutch Words

In the captivating realm of public speaking, where words hold immense power, lies the challenge of reducing the use of crutch words. But let us transcend the ordinary and embark on a unique and creative journey that liberates your language from the clutches of filler words. Prepare to unleash your linguistic prowess and captivate your audience with a seamless flow of confident and impactful speech.

Imagine your words as brushstrokes on a canvas, each one carefully chosen to create a masterpiece of communication. Embrace the power of conscious awareness and mindfulness, for these are the keys to unlocking the gateways to eloquence. As you embark on this journey, let us explore unique and creative strategies to reduce the use of crutch words and elevate your language to new heights.

Strategy 1:

Embrace the Power of Pauses

Imagine a moment of silence hanging in the air, like a pregnant pause pregnant with anticipation. Harness the power of pauses to gather your thoughts, create emphasis, and allow your words to resonate with your audience. Embrace the art of strategic silence, as it not only reduces the need for crutch words but also adds depth and impact to your speech.

Strategy 2:
Amplify Your Vocabulary

Picture your vocabulary as a treasure trove of words waiting to be discovered. Expand your linguistic repertoire by actively seeking out new words and phrases that convey your intended meaning with precision and eloquence. Immerse yourself in literature, explore diverse genres, and cultivate a love for language. By enriching your vocabulary, you equip yourself with a vast arsenal of alternatives, reducing the reliance on crutch words.

Strategy 3:
Practice Mindful Speaking

Envision yourself as a conductor of words, observing each syllable and phrase with mindful attention. Cultivate self-awareness and catch yourself in the act of using crutch words. As you become attuned to their presence, gently replace them with purposeful pauses, varied sentence structures, or more impactful language choices. With practice, your speech will flow effortlessly, free from the burden of repetitive filler words.

Strategy 4:
Harness the Power of Gestures

Imagine your body as an extension of your words, using gestures to enhance your communication. Embrace the art of nonverbal expression to supplement your speech, conveying meaning and emphasis through intentional movements. By channeling your energy into purposeful gestures, you redirect the urge to fill the gaps with crutch words, creating a more dynamic and engaging presentation.

Strategy 5:

Embody Confidence and Poise

Picture yourself standing tall, radiating confidence and poise. Embrace the belief in your own abilities as a speaker, for confidence breeds clarity. By cultivating a strong presence and a belief in your message, you reduce the need for filler words as you deliver your thoughts with conviction and authority.

Strategy 6:

Utilize Visualization Techniques

Imagine yourself delivering a flawless speech, effortlessly weaving your words together. Before each presentation, take a moment to visualize yourself speaking with clarity, precision, and without the need for crutch words. Envision the audience hanging on to your every word, captivated by your eloquence. By visualizing success, you program your mind for a more confident and fluid delivery.

Remember, dear speaker, that the mastery of language is a lifelong pursuit. Embrace the power of pauses, amplify your vocabulary, practice mindful speaking, harness nonverbal communication, embody confidence, and utilize visualization techniques to reduce the use of crutch words. The path to eloquence is paved with intention, awareness, and the unwavering desire to craft your words with purpose.

So, fellow wordsmith, let us embark on this creative journey together. Liberate your language from the grip of crutch words, unleashing a flow of eloquence that captivates and inspires. Are you ready to paint a masterpiece of communication, where each word holds significance and impact? The world eagerly awaits the unique and captivating expression of your voice, free from the confines of filler words.

CHAPTER 15

The Art of Expressive Movement: Unleashing Body Language Mastery

In the captivating realm of public speaking, where words intertwine with gestures, lies the art of practicing great body language. But let us transcend the ordinary and embark on a unique and creative journey that elevates your physical presence to new heights. Prepare to unleash the power of your body as a captivating instrument of communication, captivating your audience with a symphony of expressive movement.

Imagine your body as a canvas upon which your thoughts and emotions come to life. Embrace the power of nonverbal communication and use your body as a medium to amplify and enhance your spoken words. As you embark on this journey, let us explore unique and creative strategies to practice great body language, captivating your audience with every gesture.

Strategy 1:

Harness the Power of Posture

Envision yourself standing tall, with shoulders back and head held high. Embrace the power of good posture as the foundation of confident body language. By aligning your body in a strong and upright position, you project an image of authority and presence. Embody the essence of self-assuredness, and watch as your audience responds to your commanding physical presence.

Strategy 2:
Embrace Gesture as a Language

Imagine your hands as extensions of your words, using gestures to emphasize and illustrate your ideas. Embrace the art of purposeful movement, allowing your hands to punctuate key points, convey emotion, and create visual imagery. Experiment with the range and intensity of your gestures, adapting them to the tone and content of your speech. By using gestures effectively, you bring your words to life, captivating your audience through visual communication.

Strategy 3:
Utilize Facial Expressions

Picture your face as a canvas of emotions, capable of conveying a multitude of feelings without uttering a single word. Embrace the power of facial expressions to match the tone and message of your speech. Smile to create warmth and approachability, furrow your brow to show concern or seriousness, and raise an eyebrow to express curiosity or intrigue. Through your facial expressions, you forge a deeper connection with your audience, amplifying the impact of your words.

Strategy 4:
Move with Purpose

Envision yourself moving across the stage with purpose and intention. Embrace the power of intentional movement to engage your audience and emphasize key points. Take confident strides, glide gracefully, or even pause to create moments of stillness that command attention. By using movement strategically, you create a dynamic and visually captivating performance that enhances your message.

Strategy 5:
Use Space to Your Advantage

Imagine the stage as your playground, an open canvas for creative expression. Embrace the power of spatial awareness and use the stage to your advantage. Explore different areas, positions, and levels to enhance the visual impact of your presentation. Take a step forward to assert a point, step back to create anticipation, or even move among the audience to foster connection and engagement. By utilizing space creatively, you create a captivating visual experience for your audience.

Strategy 6:
Practice Mirror Exercises

Picture yourself in front of a mirror, observing your own body language. Engage in mirror exercises to refine your movements, gestures, and facial expressions. Experiment with different postures, gestures, and expressions, observing how they contribute to your overall delivery. By practicing in front of a mirror, you cultivate self-awareness and refine your body language to be more effective and impactful.

Remember, dear speaker, that your body is a powerful instrument of communication. Embrace the power of posture, gesture, facial expressions, purposeful movement, spatial awareness, and mirror exercises to practice great body language. The art of expressive movement will elevate your presence, captivate your audience, and add a new dimension to your spoken words.

So, fellow master of movement, let us embark on this creative journey together. Explore the artistry of body language, using your physical presence to convey meaning, emotion, and connection. Are you ready to captivate your audience through the captivating symphony of your unique and creative body language? The stage is set, and the world eagerly awaits the eloquence of your expressive movement.

CHAPTER 16

Beyond Words: Unleashing Power with Props and Visual Aids

In the captivating realm of public speaking, where words intertwine with visual elements, lies the art of using props and visual aids. But let us transcend the ordinary and embark on a unique and creative journey that elevates your presentations to new heights. Prepare to unleash the power of props and visual aids, captivating your audience with a multi-sensory experience that goes beyond words alone.

Imagine your words as threads, and props and visual aids as colorful tapestries woven into your speech. Embrace the power of visual communication and use these tools to enhance, clarify, and reinforce your message. As you embark on this journey, let us explore unique and creative strategies to use props and visual aids, captivating your audience with an immersive and memorable experience.

Strategy 1:

The Power of Visual Metaphors

Imagine holding in your hands a symbol that represents an abstract concept. Embrace the power of visual metaphors by using props that embody the essence of your message. A puzzle piece to represent unity, a compass to symbolize direction, or a lightbulb to convey an idea. These visual metaphors add depth, intrigue, and visual impact to your speech, engaging your audience on a deeper level.

Strategy 2:
Unleash the Power of Demonstration

Envision yourself demonstrating a process or a concept with the aid of props. Embrace the power of hands-on experiences to engage your audience and make your message come alive. Whether it's a physical demonstration, a product prototype, or a simple model, props allow your audience to witness and understand your message in a tangible and memorable way.

Strategy 3:
Visualize Data with Infographics

Picture your data transformed into visually appealing and easily digestible infographics. Embrace the power of visualizing complex information through charts, graphs, and diagrams. By presenting data in a visual format, you make it more accessible and memorable for your audience. Engage their visual senses and create a connection between the numbers and the story they tell.

Strategy 4:
Embrace Multimedia Presentations

Imagine incorporating multimedia elements into your presentations. Embrace the power of technology to enhance your message with images, videos, animations, or sound effects. These dynamic visual aids captivate your audience's attention and add an extra layer of engagement. Use multimedia strategically to complement and reinforce your spoken words, creating a cohesive and impactful presentation.

Strategy 5:
Props as Storytelling Tools

Envision props as storytelling companions that bring your narrative to life. Embrace the power of using objects, artifacts, or images that evoke emotions and vivid imagery. A personal item that represents a significant moment, a historical artifact that transports your audience to a different era, or a photograph that captures the essence of a story. By incorporating props into your storytelling, you create a powerful and immersive experience for your listeners.

Strategy 6:
Creative Visual Displays

Picture a visually stunning display that adds a touch of creativity and flair to your presentation. Embrace the power of aesthetics by arranging your props and visual aids in an artistic and visually pleasing manner. Use colors, textures, and creative layouts to captivate your audience's attention and create a memorable visual experience that enhances your message.

Remember, dear speaker, that props and visual aids are tools that enhance and amplify your message. Embrace the power of visual metaphors, demonstrations, infographics, multimedia presentations, storytelling props, and creative displays to captivate your audience on a multi-sensory level. By combining the power of words with captivating visual elements, you create a presentation that lingers in the minds and hearts of your listeners.

So, fellow visual conductor, let us embark on this creative journey together. Explore the endless possibilities of props and visual aids, transforming your presentations into immersive experiences that transcend words alone. Are you ready to captivate your audience with a unique and creative visual feast that accompanies your spoken words? The stage is set, and the world eagerly awaits the multi-dimensional impact of your presentation.

CHAPTER 16

Navigating the Technological Maze: Unleashing Strategies to Anticipate and Overcome Tech Mishaps

In the captivating realm of public speaking, where technology and communication intertwine, lies the inevitable presence of tech mishaps. But let us transcend the ordinary and embark on a unique and creative journey that empowers you to navigate the technological maze with grace and confidence. Prepare to unleash the power of anticipation and resilience, captivating your audience even when faced with unexpected tech challenges.

Imagine yourself as a tech-savvy magician, ready to turn potential mishaps into opportunities for innovation and connection. Embrace the power of proactive planning and creative problem-solving, ensuring a seamless experience for both you and your audience. As you embark on this journey, let us explore unique and creative strategies to anticipate and overcome tech mishaps, transforming challenges into moments of triumph.

Strategy 1:

Tech Rehearsals and Backup Plans

Envision yourself stepping onto the virtual or physical stage, fully equipped with a comprehensive tech rehearsal and backup plans. Embrace the power of preparedness by conducting thorough run-throughs of your presentation, testing all technical aspects in advance. Have backup devices, cables, and accessories readily available to address any potential malfunctions. By rehearsing and planning for contingencies, you create a safety net that minimizes the impact of tech mishaps.

Strategy 2:
Familiarize Yourself with the Venue

Picture yourself exploring the venue, whether physical or virtual, like an adventurous explorer. Embrace the power of familiarity by understanding the technological infrastructure available to you. Get to know the audiovisual systems, lighting setups, internet connections, and any specific software or platforms you will be using. By acquainting yourself with the venue's tech landscape, you can anticipate potential issues and adapt accordingly.

Strategy 3:
Create Redundancies

Imagine building redundancies into your tech setup, like a safety net that catches you when things go awry. Embrace the power of backup options by having duplicate files, saved in multiple formats and locations. Consider having alternative presentation methods, such as printed materials or handouts, in case of technology failure. By creating redundancies, you ensure that your message can be delivered even in the face of unexpected tech challenges.

Strategy 4:
Develop Technical Troubleshooting Skills

Picture yourself as a tech guru, confident in your ability to troubleshoot and resolve technical issues on the spot. Embrace the power of technical knowledge by familiarizing yourself with common tech problems and their solutions. Learn basic troubleshooting techniques, such as restarting devices, checking connections, or adjusting settings. By developing your technical troubleshooting skills, you become more resilient and adaptable in the face of tech mishaps.

Strategy 5:

Engage with the Audience during Tech Hiccups

Envision a moment of tech hiccup turning into an opportunity for audience engagement and connection. Embrace the power of improvisation by acknowledging the issue openly and transparently with your audience. Use humor, storytelling, or interactive activities to keep the audience engaged while the tech issue is being resolved. By embracing the unexpected and engaging with your audience authentically, you transform a potential setback into a memorable and engaging experience.

Strategy 6:

Collaborate with Tech Support

Imagine yourself collaborating seamlessly with tech support, like a harmonious duet. Embrace the power of teamwork by establishing a line of communication with technical support personnel, whether they are onsite or available remotely. Familiarize them with your presentation and tech requirements, ensuring they are ready to assist if any issues arise. By collaborating with tech support, you can quickly resolve tech mishaps and maintain a smooth flow during your presentation.

Remember, dear speaker, that tech mishaps are merely opportunities for you to showcase your adaptability and resilience. Embrace the power of tech rehearsals, backup plans, venue familiarity, redundancies, troubleshooting skills, audience engagement, and collaboration with tech support. By anticipating and overcoming tech mishaps creatively, you demonstrate your professionalism and ensure a memorable and seamless experience for your audience.

So, fellow tech magician, let us embark on this creative journey together. Explore the maze of technology with confidence and poise, turning potential mishaps into moments of triumph. Are you ready to captivate your audience, even in the face of tech challenges? The stage is set, and the world eagerly awaits your creative navigation through the technological maze.

CLOSE YOUR SPEECH

CHAPTER 17

Engaging Minds: Unleashing Strategies to Handle Audience Q&A

In the captivating realm of public speaking, where minds connect and curiosity flourishes, lies the art of handling audience questions and answers. But let us transcend the ordinary and embark on a unique and creative journey that empowers you to navigate the realm of Q&A with confidence and finesse. Prepare to unleash the power of authentic engagement, captivating your audience and sparking enlightening conversations.

Imagine yourself as a skilled conductor, orchestrating a symphony of dialogue and exchange. Embrace the power of active listening, thoughtful responses, and creative approaches to make the Q&A session a memorable and enriching experience for both you and your audience. As you embark on this journey, let us explore unique and creative strategies to handle audience Q&A, fostering meaningful connections and inspiring further exploration.

Strategy 1:

Establish a Safe and Welcoming Environment

Envision yourself creating a safe and welcoming space where questions are encouraged and valued. Embrace the power of a warm and inclusive tone as you invite your audience to share their thoughts and inquiries. Foster an atmosphere of respect and openness, ensuring that everyone feels comfortable to ask questions and contribute to the discussion. By setting the stage for a positive Q&A experience, you create an environment where meaningful dialogue can thrive.

Strategy 2:

Active Listening and Empathetic Responses

Picture yourself fully present and engaged as each question is posed. Embrace the power of active listening, giving your undivided attention to each person who speaks. Demonstrate empathy and understanding in your responses, acknowledging the value of their questions and concerns. By truly hearing and empathizing with your audience, you create a connection that fosters trust and encourages further participation.

Strategy 3:

Encourage Diverse Perspectives

Imagine embracing the diversity of your audience and their unique perspectives. Embrace the power of inclusivity by encouraging questions from individuals with different backgrounds, experiences, and viewpoints. Create an environment where everyone feels seen and valued, and where a range of perspectives can enrich the discussion. By fostering diverse participation, you create a Q&A session that reflects the richness and complexity of the topic at hand.

Strategy 4:

Spark Creativity with Thought-Provoking Questions

Envision yourself igniting a spark of curiosity and creativity with thought-provoking questions. Embrace the power of well-crafted questions to inspire deeper thinking and generate meaningful discussion. Pose open-ended inquiries that invite the audience to share their insights and explore new perspectives. By asking thought-provoking questions, you invite your audience to become active participants in the conversation, transforming the Q&A session into a collective journey of discovery.

Strategy 5:

Incorporate Multimedia and Visual Aids

Picture yourself using visual aids or multimedia elements to enhance your responses. Embrace the power of visual communication by incorporating relevant images, charts, or videos that support your answers. These visual aids not only provide clarity but also add an extra layer of engagement to the Q&A session. By utilizing multimedia creatively, you create a dynamic and visually captivating experience that enhances the understanding and impact of your responses.

Strategy 6:

End on a Positive and Inspiring Note

Imagine concluding the Q&A session on a positive and inspiring note, leaving your audience feeling inspired and empowered. Embrace the power of a thoughtful and uplifting closing remark that summarizes key insights or highlights from the discussion. Express gratitude for the audience's participation and encourage them to continue exploring the topic further. By ending the Q&A session on a positive and inspiring note, you leave a lasting impression and ensure a sense of fulfillment for both you and your audience.

Remember, dear speaker, that the Q&A session is a valuable opportunity to engage with your audience, foster connections, and inspire further exploration. Embrace the power of a safe and welcoming environment, active listening, diverse perspectives, thought-provoking questions, visual aids, and a positive closing. By handling audience Q&A in a unique and creative way, you create a memorable and enriching experience for all involved.

So, fellow conductor of dialogue, let us embark on this creative journey together. Explore the artistry of handling audience questions and answers with confidence and finesse. Are you ready to captivate your audience with engaging Q&A sessions that ignite minds and foster meaningful connections? The stage is set, and the world eagerly awaits the enlightening symphony of your unique and creative Q&A handling.

CHAPTER 18

The Final Flourish: Unleashing Ways to Close Your Speech

In the captivating realm of public speaking, where words resonate and emotions linger, lies the art of closing your speech with impact and grace. But let us transcend the ordinary and embark on a unique and creative journey that empowers you to leave a lasting impression on your audience. Prepare to unleash the power of a powerful conclusion, captivating your listeners and inspiring them to take action.

Imagine yourself as a master storyteller, crafting the final chapter of your speech with precision and artistry. Embrace the power of a strong and memorable closing that leaves your audience with a sense of fulfillment and a desire for more. As you embark on this journey, let us explore unique and creative ways to close your speech, elevating your message and leaving a lasting imprint on the hearts and minds of your listeners.

Strategy 1:
The Call to Action

Envision yourself igniting a spark of motivation and action in your audience. Embrace the power of a compelling call to action that challenges and inspires your listeners to make a change. Whether it's urging them to support a cause, embrace a new perspective, or take concrete steps towards a goal, a well-crafted call to action ignites their passion and empowers them to make a difference.

Strategy 2:
The Thought-Provoking Question

Picture yourself leaving your audience pondering with a thought-provoking question. Embrace the power of an intriguing inquiry that lingers in their minds, encouraging them to reflect and explore further. Pose a question that challenges their assumptions, sparks curiosity, or invites them to consider a new perspective. By leaving them with a question to ponder, you inspire ongoing contemplation and engagement with your message.

Strategy 3:
The Inspiring Story or Anecdote

Imagine sharing a powerful story or anecdote that encapsulates the essence of your message. Embrace the power of storytelling to leave a lasting emotional impact on your audience. Craft a narrative that evokes empathy, sparks inspiration, or highlights the transformative power of your message. By sharing a compelling story, you connect with your audience on a deeper level, leaving them inspired and moved.

Strategy 4:
The Poignant Quotation

Envision yourself leaving your audience with a memorable quotation that encapsulates the core message of your speech. Embrace the power of a well-chosen quote that resonates with your audience and reinforces the key ideas you've presented. Select a quotation from a respected figure, a literary masterpiece, or even a popular culture reference that adds depth and memorability to your closing remarks.

Strategy 5:
The Visual Metaphor

Picture yourself using a visual metaphor to create a powerful closing image in the minds of your audience. Embrace the power of evocative imagery by employing a symbolic object, gesture, or visual representation that encapsulates your main idea. Use this metaphor to evoke emotion, create a lasting visual impression, and reinforce your message in a unique and memorable way.

Strategy 6:
The Call Back to the Opening

Imagine circling back to your opening remarks, creating a sense of closure and unity in your speech. Embrace the power of referencing your opening story, anecdote, or theme to bring your speech full circle. By reconnecting with your audience's initial engagement, you create a sense of completeness and reinforce the journey you've taken together. This closing technique leaves your audience with a sense of satisfaction and a feeling of a well-rounded experience.

Remember, dear speaker, that the closing of your speech is your final opportunity to leave a lasting impression and inspire action. Embrace the power of a strong call to action, thought-provoking questions, inspiring stories, poignant quotations, visual metaphors, and callbacks to the opening. By closing your speech in a unique and creative way, you create a lasting impact that resonates with your audience long after the words have been spoken.

So, fellow master of words, let us embark on this creative journey together. Explore the artistry of closing your speech with impact and grace, leaving an indelible imprint on your audience. Are you ready to captivate your listeners with a closing that lingers in their hearts and minds? The stage is set, and the world eagerly awaits the final flourish of your unique and creative speech closure.

CHAPTER 19

The Echo of Growth: Unleashing Ways to Get Feedback on Your Speaking

In the captivating realm of public speaking, where growth and refinement take center stage, lies the art of seeking feedback to elevate your speaking skills. But let us transcend the ordinary and embark on a unique and creative journey that empowers you to gather feedback in a way that is both insightful and inspiring. Prepare to unleash the power of constructive critique, guiding you towards continuous improvement and mastery.

Imagine yourself as an architect of your own development, designing a feedback ecosystem that nurtures growth and fuels your progress. Embrace the power of unique and creative methods to gather feedback, transforming the process into a rich and rewarding experience. As you embark on this journey, let us explore innovative strategies to obtain feedback on your speaking, opening doors to new insights and possibilities.

Strategy 1:
The Expressive Arts

Envision yourself harnessing the power of artistic expression to gather feedback. Embrace the creative arts, such as painting, sketching, or even interpretive dance, as vehicles for receiving feedback. Invite others to visually represent their impressions of your speech through their chosen art form. The result? A unique and immersive feedback experience that taps into the depths of human creativity and provides fresh perspectives on your speaking.

Strategy 2:

The Collaborative Workshop

Picture yourself creating a collaborative workshop where participants engage in interactive activities to provide feedback. Embrace the power of group dynamics and collective wisdom by facilitating exercises that encourage constructive critique and open dialogue. Create a safe space where individuals can share their observations, insights, and suggestions. By fostering a collaborative environment, you tap into the collective intelligence of your peers, enriching your understanding of your speaking abilities.

Strategy 3:

The Storytelling Circle

Imagine gathering a group of individuals for a storytelling circle, where they share their own stories and reflections inspired by your speech. Embrace the power of storytelling as a means of providing feedback. Each participant can share their personal experiences, emotions, and takeaways, offering valuable insights into the impact of your words. By fostering a space for shared narratives, you gain a deeper understanding of how your message resonates and can refine your storytelling prowess.

Strategy 4:

The Multimedia Showcase

Envision creating a multimedia showcase where attendees can provide feedback through various creative mediums. Embrace the power of technology and multimedia platforms to gather feedback in innovative ways. Invite participants to submit videos, audio recordings, or visual presentations that capture their thoughts and impressions of your speaking. By embracing diverse forms of feedback, you receive a multi-dimensional perspective that enhances your self-awareness and growth.

Strategy 5:

The Gamified Evaluation

Picture yourself transforming the feedback process into a game-like experience. Embrace the power of gamification by creating interactive evaluation activities that engage your audience. Design a scoring system, challenges, or quizzes related to your speaking performance. Encourage participants to provide feedback through gameplay, making the process enjoyable and stimulating for both them and yourself. By gamifying the evaluation, you inject an element of fun and excitement into the feedback process.

Strategy 6:

The Immersive Simulation

Imagine immersing yourself in a simulated speaking environment where you can receive real-time feedback. Embrace the power of technology to recreate speaking scenarios, such as virtual reality or simulated presentations. Engage with a virtual audience that provides feedback on your speaking performance, allowing you to practice and refine your skills in a controlled yet realistic setting. By immersing yourself in these simulated experiences, you gain valuable insights that propel your growth as a speaker.

Remember, dear speaker, that seeking feedback is a transformative act that fuels your growth and development. Embrace the power of expressive arts, collaborative workshops, storytelling circles, multimedia showcases, gamified evaluations, and immersive simulations. By seeking feedback in unique and creative ways, you create a feedback ecosystem that expands your horizons and propels you towards speaking mastery.

So, fellow seeker of growth, let us embark on this creative journey together. Explore the artistry of gathering feedback in innovative and inspiring ways, nurturing your speaking abilities and refining your craft. Are you ready to unlock new dimensions of insight and possibilities? The stage is set, and the world eagerly awaits the echo of growth created by your unique and creative feedback-seeking endeavors.

Conclusion:

As we come to the final notes of this symphony of public speaking, let us reflect on the transformative journey we have embarked upon. Throughout this book, we have delved into the depths of creativity, exploring unique and innovative approaches to captivate audiences, inspire change, and leave a lasting impact. Now, it is time to conclude our harmonious exploration with a flourish of creativity and inspiration.

Dear conductor of words, you hold within you the power to unleash your voice and ignite the world. The stage is set, and the spotlight awaits your command. By embracing your creativity and infusing it into your public speaking, you have the ability to transcend the ordinary and create extraordinary moments of connection, understanding, and influence.

Remember that each chapter of this book has been a stepping stone towards unlocking your full potential as a speaker. From identifying your audience with the curiosity of an explorer, to crafting your message with the finesse of an artist, to engaging in the dance of feedback with the spirit of a collaborator, you have honed your skills and expanded your horizons.

Embrace the uniqueness that resides within you. Allow it to shape your presence, fuel your authenticity, and guide your delivery. Embrace the power of storytelling, metaphor, and visualization to transport your audience to new realms of imagination and inspiration. Let your voice be a catalyst for change, a beacon of hope, and a force for transformation.

In this book, we have not only explored the foundations of public speaking but have also pushed the boundaries of what is possible. We have challenged conventions, unleashed creativity, and celebrated the artistry of communication. The journey does not end here. It is only the beginning of your lifelong quest to continually refine and evolve as a speaker.

So, as you step onto the grand stage of life, remember the lessons you have learned, the insights you have gained, and the unique voice that only you possess. Embrace the power of creativity, authenticity, and connection to weave a symphony of words that resonates with hearts and minds.

Dear reader, the world eagerly awaits your voice, your story, and your message. Let this book be your guiding companion as you embrace the challenges, the triumphs, and the endless possibilities that lie ahead. Unleash your voice, ignite the world, and become the maestro of your own speaking journey.

Now, go forth and let your words ripple through the universe, for the world is your stage, and you are the conductor of change.

CONCLUSION

As we come to the final notes of this symphony of public speaking, let us reflect on the transformative journey we have embarked upon. Throughout this book, we have delved into the depths of creativity, exploring unique and innovative approaches to captivate audiences, inspire change, and leave a lasting impact. Now, it is time to conclude our harmonious exploration with a flourish of creativity and inspiration.

Dear conductor of words, you hold within you the power to unleash your voice and ignite the world. The stage is set, and the spotlight awaits your command. By embracing your creativity and infusing it into your public speaking, you have the ability to transcend the ordinary and create extraordinary moments of connection, understanding, and influence.

Remember that each chapter of this book has been a stepping stone towards unlocking your full potential as a speaker. From identifying your audience with the curiosity of an explorer, to crafting your message with the finesse of an artist, to engaging in the dance of feedback with the spirit of a collaborator, you have honed your skills and expanded your horizons.

Embrace the uniqueness that resides within you. Allow it to shape your presence, fuel your authenticity, and guide your delivery. Embrace the power of storytelling, metaphor, and visualization to transport your audience to new realms of imagination and inspiration. Let your voice be a catalyst for change, a beacon of hope, and a force for transformation.

In this book, we have not only explored the foundations of public speaking but have also pushed the boundaries of what is possible. We have challenged conventions, unleashed creativity, and celebrated the artistry of communication. The journey does not end here. It is only the beginning of your lifelong quest to continually refine and evolve as a speaker.

So, as you step onto the grand stage of life, remember the lessons you have learned, the insights you have gained, and the unique voice that only you possess. Embrace the power of creativity, authenticity, and connection to weave a symphony of words that resonates with hearts and minds.

Dear reader, the world eagerly awaits your voice, your story, and your message. Let this book be your guiding companion as you embrace the challenges, the triumphs, and the endless possibilities that lie ahead. Unleash your voice, ignite the world, and become the maestro of your own speaking journey.

Now, go forth and let your words ripple through the universe, for the world is your stage, and you are the conductor of change.

EPILOGUE

Welcome, dear reader, to a journey that will unlock the transformative power of your voice and elevate your public speaking to new heights. Within the pages of this book, I invite you to immerse yourself in the artistry of communication and explore the untapped realms of creativity that lie within you.

Public speaking is not merely a skill to be mastered; it is a form of self-expression that has the potential to inspire, influence, and ignite change. In a world where attention spans waver and information overload prevails, it is crucial to embrace unique and creative approaches to captivate your audience and leave a lasting impact.

The purpose of this book is not to provide a formulaic approach to public speaking, but rather to serve as a catalyst for your own creative exploration. Each chapter will invite you to reimagine the fundamental aspects of public speaking through a lens of innovation and originality. We will venture beyond traditional boundaries, challenging conventional wisdom and empowering you to infuse your speeches with a distinctive and memorable voice.

Drawing upon my own experiences as a speaker and communicator, as well as the wisdom of great orators, artists, and thinkers throughout history, we will uncover the secrets of effective communication and tap into the infinite reservoir of creativity that resides within you. Together, we will explore unique techniques to identify your audience, craft compelling messages, master your delivery, and forge a genuine connection with your listeners.

Throughout this book, you will encounter thought-provoking exercises, inspiring anecdotes, and practical tips to help you embrace your own creative potential. I encourage you to embark on this journey with an open mind and a willingness to step outside your comfort zone. Embrace the unexpected, challenge your assumptions, and let your imagination soar.

Remember, this book is not a definitive guide, but rather an invitation to co-create and co-discover the art of public speaking. Your voice is unique, and the world awaits your distinct perspective. By embracing the artistry of public speaking and infusing it with your creative spirit, you have the power to inspire, entertain, and transform.

As you embark on this journey, I encourage you to embrace vulnerability, embrace failure as a stepping stone to growth, and embrace your authentic self. Let your words become a symphony that resonates in the hearts and minds of your audience. Together, let us unleash the power of unique and creative expression and elevate the art of public speaking to new horizons.

So, dear reader, prepare to embark on a remarkable expedition. Embrace the artistry of public speaking and discover the limitless possibilities that lie within. The stage is set, the audience awaits, and your voice is ready to soar. Let us begin this prelude to unique and creative expression.

Fahaz Hameed

AFTERWORD

As we reach the end of this captivating book, I invite you to take a moment to reflect on the incredible journey we have embarked upon together. We have explored the depths of unique and creative expression in public speaking, unlocking the power of your voice and igniting a spark that will forever illuminate your path.

In this afterword, let us celebrate the progress you have made and acknowledge that your journey as a speaker is an ongoing symphony—a continuous evolution of growth, exploration, and refinement. As you step off the stage and into the world, remember that the principles and insights shared within these pages will forever be your trusted companions.

The essence of unique and creative expression lies not only in the techniques and strategies you have learned, but also in your commitment to authenticity and connection. You have discovered that the true magic of public speaking lies in the ability to convey your message with passion, sincerity, and an unwavering belief in the power of your words.

Embracing unique and creative expression means embracing your own story, your own style, and your own voice. It means having the courage to share your ideas, opinions, and experiences with the world, knowing that your perspective matters and has the potential to create ripples of change.

As you continue your journey, remember that every opportunity to speak is an opportunity for growth and impact. Whether you find yourself addressing a small group or commanding a grand stage, approach each speaking engagement with a sense of purpose and a commitment to delivering your message in a way that is uniquely you.

But beyond the confines of the stage, let your voice be heard in all aspects of your life. Embrace every conversation, every presentation, and every interaction as an opportunity to express yourself authentically and creatively. Remember that the principles of unique and creative expression in public speaking extend far beyond formal settings—they permeate every aspect of human connection.

As you navigate the vast landscape of public speaking, embrace the role of a lifelong learner. Seek out new insights, techniques, and perspectives. Attend workshops, watch inspiring speeches, and engage in meaningful conversations that fuel your passion and deepen your understanding of the art.

And as you continue to refine your skills and discover new dimensions of your voice, don't forget the power of mentorship. Share your experiences, knowledge, and wisdom with aspiring speakers who are just beginning their own journey. Lift others up, inspire them to embrace their own unique expression, and foster a community of creative communicators.

Dear reader, as we conclude this book, I want to express my deepest gratitude for joining me on this extraordinary exploration of unique and creative expression in public speaking. It is my sincere hope that the insights, exercises, and stories shared within these pages have ignited a fire within you—a fire that will continue to burn brightly as you embark on a future filled with captivating speeches and profound connections.

Remember that your voice has the power to change lives, to challenge norms, and to inspire greatness. Embrace your voice, nurture it, and let it reverberate through the hearts and minds of all who listen.

This afterword marks not an end, but a new beginning. May you continue to embrace the symphony of unique and creative expression in all your endeavors, and may your voice continue to touch lives and shape the world in extraordinary ways.

Thank you, dear reader, for being a part of this incredible journey. Now, go forth and let your unique and creative expression be the guiding force that propels you towards greatness.

Fahaz Hameed

ABOUT THE AUTHOR

Fahaz Hameed

Fahaz Hameed is a passionate writer who believes in the transformative power of words. Born with a love for storytelling and a curious mind, Fahaz embarked on a journey of self-discovery through writing. While pursuing a medical education, Fahaz realized that his true calling lay in the world of words and creativity.

After completing an associate's degree in communication from the University of Washington, Fahaz's passion for writing took flight. He began exploring various styles and genres, experimenting with personal narratives, informative pieces, and thought-provoking essays. Fahaz's writing journey led him to platforms like Medium, where he shares his ideas and engages with a vibrant community of readers and fellow writers.

Fahaz's writing style is characterized by a unique blend of creativity, introspection, and a desire to explore the depths of human existence. He delves into the intricacies of life, weaving together philosophical insights, personal experiences, and thought-provoking observations. Through his writing, Fahaz invites readers to join him on a journey of self-reflection and discovery, offering them a fresh perspective on the tapestry of life.

When Fahaz is not lost in the world of words, he can be found indulging in his other passions, such as exploring nature, immersing himself in art and music, and spending quality time with loved ones. He is an avid reader, constantly seeking inspiration from the works of great thinkers and storytellers. You can find Fahaz's articles on Medium, where he shares his unique perspectives and engages with readers on a wide range of topics. Connect with Fahaz on medium (@fahazhameed) to stay updated on his latest writings.
With an insatiable curiosity and a passion for writing, Fahaz

continues to explore the depths of human experience, seeking to unravel the mysteries of life through his words.

www.ingramcontent.com/pod-product-compliance
Lightning Source LLC
Chambersburg PA
CBHW040319220526
45473CB00009B/2488